MOON SPELLS FOR BEGINNERS

A step-by-step guide to moon magic, spells, lunar phases and rituals

Noel Danice

Moon spells for beginners

Moon spells for beginners

Table of Contents

INTRODUCTION

The moon (various definitions and descriptions).

The moon, also called Luna, is the regular primary satellite of the earth. It was made 4.6 billion years prior, and it is generally acknowledged that it was made when earth slammed into a planet-sized article called Theia. It is the fifth-biggest moon in our nearby planet group and is the second most brilliant article in the sky (after the sun).

History of The Moon

Called Luna by the Romans, Selene, and Artemis by the Greeks, and numerous different names in different legends. The moon has been known since ancient occasions. It is the second most splendid article in the sky after the sun. As the Moon circles around the Earth one time each month, the point between the earth, the moon, and the sun transforms; we consider this the pattern of the moon's stages. The time between progressive new moons is 29.5 days (709 hours), marginally not quite the same as the moon's orbital period (estimated against the stars) since the earth moves a colossal distance in its circle around the sun in that time. Because of its size and organization, the moon has delegated an earthbound planet alongside Mercury, Venus, Earth, and Mars.

The moon was first visited by the Soviet space apparatus Luna 2 in 1959. It is the main extraterrestrial body to have been seen by people.

The principal arrival was on July 20, 1969 (do you recollect where you were?); the latter was in December 1972. The moon is likewise the main body from which tests have been gotten back to earth. In the late spring of 1994, the moon was broadly planned by the little space apparatus Clementine and again in 1999 by Lunar Prospector. The gravitational powers between the earth and the moon cause some intriguing impacts. The clearest are the tides. The moon's gravitational fascination is more grounded on the planet closest to the moon and more vulnerable on the contrary side. Since the earth, and especially the seas, isn't wholly unbending, it is loosened up along the line toward the moon. According to our viewpoint on the earth's surface, we see two little lumps, one toward the moon and one straightforwardly inverse. The impact is more grounded in the seawater than the strong covering, so the water swells are higher.

What's more, because the earth turns a lot quicker than the moon moves in its circle, the lumps move around the planet about once a day, giving two elevated tides each day. (This is extraordinarily improved on the model; genuine waves, particularly close to the coasts, are significantly more convoluted.) But the earth isn't liquid. The earth's pivot conveys the earth's swells somewhat in front of the point straightforwardly underneath the moon. This implies that the power between the world and the moon isn't actually along the line between their focuses delivering a force on the earth and speeding up the strength on the moon. This causes a net exchange of rotational energy from the ground to the moon, dialing back the earth's pivot by around 1.5 milliseconds/century and raising the moon into a higher circle by approximately 3.8 centimeters each year.

(The contrary impact happens to satellites with surprising circles like Phobos and Triton). The uneven idea of this gravitational connection is also answerable for how the moon turns simultaneously, i.e., it is a secured stage with its circle, so a similar side is continually pointing toward the earth. Similarly, as the earth's turn is presently being eased back by the Moons impact, in the far-off past, the Moons revolution was eased back by the earth's activity, yet all things considered, the effect was a lot more grounded. When the Moons turn rate was reduced back to coordinate with its orbital period (to such an extent that the lump consistently pointed toward the earth), there could have been no topsy turvy force on the moon, and a steady circumstance accomplished. The same thing has happened to the more significant part of different satellites in the nearby planet group. Ultimately, the earth's turn will be eased back to coordinate with the moon's time frame, as well, just like the case with Pluto and Charon.

The moon seems to wobble a little (because of its marginally non-round circle), so a few levels of the far side can be seen now and then. However, most of the far side (left) was obscure until the Soviet shuttle Luna 3 captured it in 1959. (Note: there is no clouded side of the moon; all pieces of the moon get daylight a fraction of the time (except for a couple of profound cavities close to the shafts). A few employments of the term clouded side in the past may have alluded to the far side as dim in the feeling of obscure (e.g., haziest Africa), yet even that significance is as of now not substantial today!) The moon has no air. Yet, proof from Clementine proposed that there might be water ice in some profound pits close to the Moon south pole, which are for all time concealed. This has now been built up by information from Lunar Prospector. There is ice at the north pole too. The moon covers midpoints 68 km thick and changes from 0 under Mare Crisium to 107 km north of the cavity Korolev on the lunar far side. Profoundly (about 340 km span and 2% of the Moons mass).

In contrast to the earth, be that as it may, the Moons inside are not dynamic. Inquisitively, the Moons focus of mass is counterbalanced from its mathematical focus by around 2 km toward the path toward the earth. Additionally, the covering is slenderer close to the side.

There are two essential sorts of territory on the moon: the intensely cratered and ancient high countries and the generally smooth and more youthful maria. The maria (around 16% of the moon's surface) are colossal effect holes subsequently overwhelmed by liquid magma. A large portion of the surface is covered with regolith, a combination of fine residue, rough debris, and jetsam delivered by meteor impacts. Inexplicably, the maria are focused on the close to the side. Many of the pits on the side are named for famous figures throughout science like Tycho, Copernicus, and Ptolemaeus. Elements on the far side have more current references like Apollo, Gagarin, and Korolev (with a particularly Russian inclination since the primary pictures were acquired by Luna 3).

Notwithstanding the natural elements on the close to the side, the moon additionally has the colossal cavities South Pole-Aitken on the far side, which is 2250 km in breadth and 12 km profound, having it the enormous effect bowl in the planetary group and Orientale on the western appendage (as seen from earth; in the focal point of the picture at left) which is a mind-blowing illustration of a multi-ring pit. A sum of 382 kg of rock tests was gotten back to the earth by the Apollo and Luna programs. These give the more significant part of our nitty-gritty information on the moon. They are essential in that they can be dated. Indeed, even today, researchers concentrate on these valuable examples over 30 years after the last Moon landing.

Most shakes on the outer layer of the moon appear to be somewhere in the range of 4.6 and 3 billion years of age. This is an accidental match with the most seasoned earthly shakes, infrequently multiple billion years of age. Accordingly, the moon proves the early history of the Solar System not accessible on the earth. Before the investigation of the Apollo tests, there was no agreement about the beginning of the moon. There were three head speculations: co-gradual addition, which declared that the Moon and the Earth framed simultaneously from the Solar Nebula; splitting, which affirmed that the moon split off of the earth; and catch, which held that the planet accordingly captured the moon-shaped somewhere else and. No part of this function, admirably. However, the new and itemized data from the Moon rocks prompted the effect hypothesis: the earth crashed into an exceptionally enormous article (as large as Mars or more), and the moon framed from the launched-out material. There are still subtleties to be worked out; however, the effect hypothesis is presently broadly acknowledged. The moon has no attractive worldwide field. However, a portion of its surface rocks displays remanent attraction, demonstrating that there may have been a beautiful worldwide field from the get-go in the Moons history. The moon's surface is presented straightforwardly to the sun-powered breeze with no environment and no attractive area. Over its 4-billion-year lifetime, numerous particles from the sun-powered current have become installed in the Moons regolith. In this way, tests of regolith returned by the Apollo missions demonstrated importance in investigations of the sun-based breeze.

Moon spells for beginners

Understanding various symbolisms of the moon.

Symbolic Moon Facts

Moon Meanings and Moon Symbolism

Enlightening and Symbolic Moon Facts: This page on representative moon realities is dedicated to the different enlightening characteristics of the moon from a philosophical/magical point of view. All through nature, we track down a procession of fiery partners: Light/Dark, Male/Female, Increase/Decrease, and so on, and the moon has her spot yet to be determined as the partner to the sun. The sun represents the friendly (male, yang) part of direction; thus, coherently, the moon unemotionally remains as the maternal (female or yin) impact. This sex affiliation is a speculation, and (similarly as with most representative implications) there are take-offs. Moon imagery in Native American clans (Navajo, Eskimo, Pueblo ring a bell), alongside African, Japanese, Maori, Teutonic, Oceania, and Sumerian-Semitic gatherings allude to the moon as a manly power. More charming than sexual orientation is how the moon uses her power and impact. She is viewed as an illuminating presence; however, she creates no light voluntarily. She is dependent upon the sun's light to (reflect) her picture to our natural eyes. This strategy for projecting light makes the moon an image of nuance. Clearness, reflection, and roundabout derivation are acquired by detached means where the sun will firmly push ahead of its blast upon a given philosophical subject; the moon delicately encases our consideration brightening our mind in a gossamer shine that is more open to obscure impressions.

"The moon doesn't battle. It assaults nobody. It doesn't stress. It doesn't attempt to smash others. It keeps to its course, yet by its actual nature, it tenderly impacts. What other body could pull a whole sea from one shore to another? The moon is dedicated to its inclination, and its power is rarely lessened".

The general effects of the moon.

There are countless beneficial things about investing energy outdoors, enjoying the daylight, getting active work, or in any event, setting up camp under the stars. That is a specific most loved diversion of mine, which gives me a lot of time to lounge around an open-air fire and gaze up at the moon in wonder. Our nearest heavenly neighbor, and our planet's cherished satellite, have been a wellspring of interest and legends for centuries since the start of mankind on earth. Nonetheless, the moon has been around significantly longer than that, more than 4 billion years, in fact, and affects life as far as we might be concerned. Since the beginning, faith in the impacts and significance of the moon have fluctuated. A few legends have been demonstrated false, even as science has tracked down extra motivations to laud our lunar sidekick. Before we can comprehend the effect that the moon has on earth, we ought to presumably discuss the monstrous impact that brought about the moon in any case. Around 4.5 billion years prior, a Mars-sized planetoid crashed into the earth and combined into a steady planet. This was a giant effect and regurgitated tremendous measures of the liquid planet's center into neighboring space. Following the impact, the flotsam and jetsam combined more than a couple million years to frame the moon as far as we might be concerned today, albeit it was a lot nearer to our planet in those days. You may not have the foggiest idea about this; however, the moon has been gradually getting away from earth for billions of years, at a current pace of roughly 4 centimeters each year.

Since its underlying arrangement, it has fostered a consistent and stable relationship with the earth, giving strength and evening glow, just as different actual impacts on our seas, biological systems, and as some believe even our state of mind! As referenced, various undeniable and exceptionally bogus cases have been made regarding our shining neighbor, and it's essential to know the distinction!

Effects of the Moon on Earth

Regarding what our intelligent moon means for our lives on earth, the significant focuses incorporate flowing movement, planetary slant, and developmental history, remembering the historical backdrop of humankind for the planet!

Tidal Activity

While the early moon was settling and hardening in earth's circle, the expanses of the planet were likewise cooling, following two or three hundred million years of post-sway shakiness. Regardless of how the moon is a lot more modest than the earth, it has a gravitational draw, and 4 billion years prior, when the moon was a large portion of the separation from the planet than it is at present, that gravitational force was fundamentally more grounded. That pull was substantially more recognizable in the world confronting the moon, just as the focal point of the planet, rather than the contrary side of the earth (facing away from the moon). Subsequently, we have tides on this planet, brought about by the protruding of water in the world confronting the moon. Elevated tides generally happen on the world's shorelines at regular intervals, trailed by low tides 6 hours after the fact. These tides used to be undeniably more outrageous when the moon was nearer to the planet, yet have lessened in the course of the last 4 billion years as the moon circles ever further away. The moon has likewise dialed back the twist of the earth significantly in the previous scarcely any million centuries. Rather than having 6-12 hours in a day, as was logical, the situation at the beginning of the earth, flowing grinding from the protruding of that seawater, has eased back the pace of our planet's turn. The moon is shortening the length consistently, yet at a minuscule pace of under 1 second like clockwork.

Planetary Tilt

This is one of the seriously fascinating and huge jobs that the moon has played in our lives. As a large portion of you know, our planet doesn't turn without a hitch, similar to marble on a tabletop. It is more like a turning top, implying that it has a slight wobble. While that doesn't sound all that steady as we tear through the universe, that wobble is vital. It furnishes us with the seasons, long periods of contrasting daylight length, and climatic locales that remain to some degree stable on a yearly or occasional premise. The moon and the earth have secured a gravitational hug, which gives solidness to both divine items. Without the moon holding us set up, our planetary pivot would move substantially more definitely, even conceivably flipping on its side, which was the destiny of Mars, bringing about enormous changes to the planet's posts. This would make presence significantly more of a battle, taking into account that the icy districts of the world could once in a while shift to the equator, as well as the other way around. Super durable settlement in specific regions would be substantially more troublesome.

Evolutionary History

The moon keeps on directing specific cycles for living creatures in the world, albeit the cases of the moon's impact on period and rates of birth have been to a great extent limited. For animals who base their Circadian rhythms on the patterns of the moon, be that as it may, connected fundamentally to the presence of light around evening time, their advancement and endurance would be affected in case the moon abruptly vanished. Since the beginning, lions, bats, creepy crawlies, and innumerable species have advanced specific practices related to the moon's presence, like mating, hunting, hibernation, and hostility. It is possible that the way of developmental history would have been different and might not have even prompted mankind as far as we might be concerned.

The Effects of Full Moon on Emotions

Balance general, the moon is associated with our enthusiastic selves. Large numbers of the full moon consequences for human conduct and feelings are concealed profound inside our psyche. In this way, when the moon is complete, it discharges energy that incredibly influences us all, actually just as aggregately. Every week that passes, the moon travels through every zodiac house, making its way from whatever garbage is in its manner. The components it clear or potentially reboot are energy vessels that are associated with our spirit. The full moon unsettles this extension that associates us inside, causing changes. A portion of these changes is inconspicuous while others are uncommon, which is why you see many carrying on of character. Generally, however, it isn't bizarre; it is their actual selves introduced to the world. To themselves or friends, this might seem, by all accounts, to be strange because the individual doesn't have the foggiest idea of how to deal with this unexpected internal change. Moreover, since the shock of energy is many solid are not profoundly and sincerely prepared to deal with it.

Moon Symbol Meaning - Water Subconscious Emotions

What's more, in the ordinary discussion, we talk about "the ocean of affection," "suffocating in pity," and contrast the profundity of our sentiments with the profoundness of the ocean. Full moons are even ideas to impact human and creature conduct, causing serious contemplations, uplifted feelings, and a few types of psychosis. Indeed, the Roman goddess of the moon is named Luna, the prefix of "insane person." The actual word comes from the Latin word "lunaticus," which initially alluded to epilepsy, franticness, and sicknesses; however, the moon is brought about.

Since the moon constantly goes through patterns of development and decay, the moon's periods are viewed as images to direct our growth and advancement.

New moon meaning: At the point when the moon is entirely dim, with no light from the sun, it is symbolic of a peaceful time - the time before something starts. It is considered an opportunity to make new arrangements or consider what ventures or dreams you wish to set into movement.

Waxing moon meaning: This moon is halfway enlightened and developing. It addresses the advancement and extension of your venture, time for you to remain roused, make a steady move and fortify your determination.

Full moon meaning: This moon is part of the way enlightened and developing. It addresses the advancement and development of your undertaking, time for you to remain propelled, make a predictable move and reinforce your purpose.

Waning moon meaning: The moon is again enlightened but is presently diminishing in size. This addresses a period of reflection, cleansing, and cleaning up. Time to relinquish individuals and things that currently don't serve you. These can be connections, negative contemplations, helpless propensities, or undertakings you are not generally intrigued by. This time of cleansing permits you to begin again with a reasonable brain to seek new ventures or objectives during the new moon.

Triple Moon Symbol Meaning

The triple moon is an image of Wiccan and Pagan customs and can be found on crowns or headpieces worn by priestesses. A goddess image addresses the Maiden, Mother, and Crone as the waxing, full and disappearing moons. It is also an image of womanliness's otherworldly parts, like instinct, clairvoyant capacities, innovativeness, and astuteness.

The Maiden, represented by the waxing moon, addresses immaculateness, energy, and charm. She is loaded with idealism, excited for fresh starts and what the future will bring.

The mother, represented by the full moon, addresses satisfaction, richness, readiness, and security. She is mindful and frequently parental, there to support and secure.

The Crone, represented by the disappearing moon, addresses intelligence, development, consummation, and peacefulness. She has a long period of involvement and mirrors the finish to all periods of life. Together, the Maiden, Mother, and Crone likewise represent the pattern of birth, life, demise, and resurrection.

Sun and Moon Meaning

The sun and the moon have been the subject of endless show-stoppers through mankind's set of experiences. There are numerous typical contrary energies on the planet - constantly, blistering and excellent, male and female, life and passing, and obviously, the sun and the moon. When the sun and moon are seen together, they address the meeting up of inverse powers, representing solidarity and participation amid variety. The sun and moon as inverse powers are frequently addressed as male and female substances. The sun is commonly seen as having customary manly characteristics - fortitude, freedom, emphatic Ness, and direction strength.

It is generally very similar - regular, it goes through the sky similarly, emitting light and hotness. It is consistent, solid, and clear, never veiling or masking itself in any capacity. Then again, the moon is viewed as having female characteristics - delicacy, affectability, empathy, and association with others. Since the moon appears to change each night, in shape and size, yet additionally in shading, it is said to run the feelings, which are flighty and change contingent upon our musings, mentalities, and the states of our lives. The sun and moon image also communicates a widespread standard of life - that where it is excellent, it is likewise awful. It recognizes the different sides of the human soul - everybody has a decent side and a terrible side. It is additionally a heartfelt image of the adoration between a man and a lady, representing a passionate and actual association. There is an excellent statement that goes, "Recount to me the tale concerning how the sun adored the moon such a lot of the kicked the bucket each night just to allow her to relax." It is a statement about sentiment and the penances we will make for those we love.

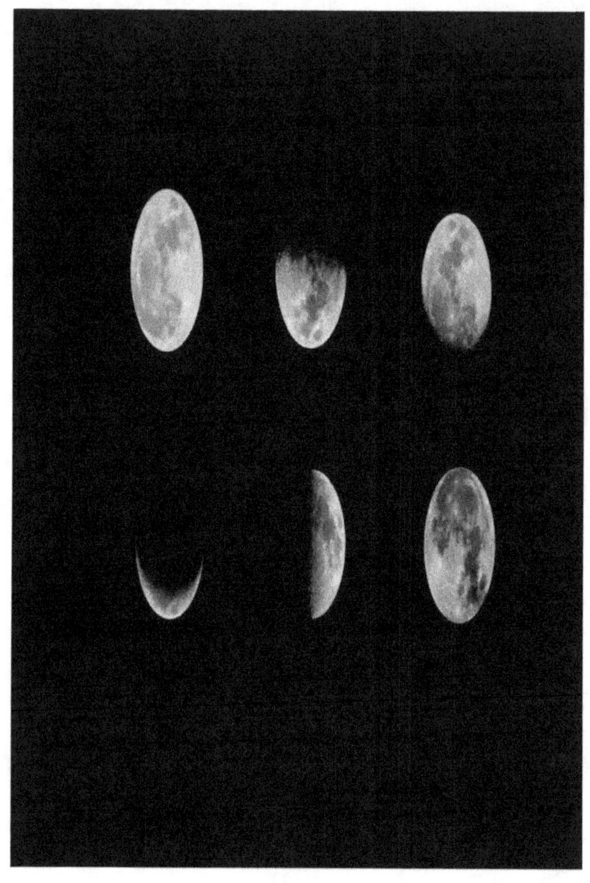

CHAPTER 2
PHASES OF THE MOON

Understanding the phases of the moon — time/period of appearance and shapes.
What Is the Moon Phase Cycle?

The perspective on the moon from the earth is continually evolving. These progressions are sorted into eight stages that rehash during each synodic month. A synodic month keeps going 29 and a half days and is the period that it takes for the moon to finish its eight-stage cycle. The picture of the moon seen from earth changes depending on the sun, moon, and earth. As the moon completes its circle around the earth, the shadow cast onto the moon changes. As the synodic month passes, the moon will seem to develop from right to left, then, at that point, when complete will start to appear to fade from right to left. The progressions in the moon stage cycle can affect a wide range of processes on earth. A notable change is a change in the sea's tides dependent on the period of the cycle. Elevated and low tides will fluctuate dependent on the situation of the moon due to the progressions in attractive energy power as the moon moves along its circle.

The moon might seem to change shape, yet the splendid surface you see and the evening glow that arrives at earth is daylight reflecting off the lunar surface. As the Moon circles our planet, its shifting position implies that the sun illuminates various locales, revealing that the moon changes shape over the long haul. An ideal method of comprehending the lunar stages is to routinely go out on a crisp evening when the moon is in the sky and notice it. For erring on this, read our aide on the best way to detect the moon. On average, 384,400km from the earth is staggering to the unaided eye and terrific through optics or a tiny telescope. It is additionally an incredible objective to photo. For inclining further toward this, read our aide on the best way to photograph the moon or our fledgling's manual for astrophotography.

The moon appears peaceful, yet it is tearing toward the east going at 3,682 km/h. Since its practically roundabout circle is tipped a simple five comparative with Earths, it pretty much follows the ecliptic (the sun's obvious way) across the sky. You might have seen that the moon consistently keeps a similar face turned towards us. It pivots once on its hub while it takes 27 days and seven hours to circle the earth. This synchronization is called flowing locking. It was an aftereffect of earth's gravitational impact on the youthful moon when it was shaping. During its curved excursion around the earth, the moon travels through stages; the term we use to portray the amount of the lunar circle seems enlightened as seen from the ground. This curved circle joined with the steps is likewise what prompts the presence of a supposed supermoon. The moon is, in every case, half-lit; we don't view it as such. Whatever stage was seen, the contrary location is going on the most distant side of the moon. And keeping in mind that we just at any point see one eliminator (the name given to the splitting line between the light and dim pieces of the lunar surface) clearing right to the left across the lunar plate whenever there are two of them circumnavigating the Moon precisely 180 separated; the morning eliminator (which introduces the lunar day) and the evening eliminator (which brings the night behind it).

The phases of the moon

Many individuals don't acknowledge (even though it's sensible) that there's likewise a connection between the Moons stages and moonrise times. There are eight absolute periods of the moon cycle, four essential, and four secondaries. The vital phases are the new moon, first quarter, full moon, and last quarter. The auxiliary phases are waxing bow, waxing gibbous, disappearing bow, and melting away gibbous. The term waxing alludes to developing the moon's picture while winding down alludes to a contracting view.

New Moon

The primary moon period of the synodic month is the new moon. This stage happens when the moon is straightforwardly between the earth and the sun. When the moon is in this situation, there is no daylight thought about the outer layer of the moon that is confronting the earth. In this stage, our satellite is imperceptible. The Sun and Moon are on a similar side of Earthrise together, yet we can't consider the moon concealed in the sun's glare. There's very little to see at any rate, as its face towards us is absolutely in shadow.

Full Moon

Partially through the morning eliminators venture, the moon is on the opposite side of the earth from the sun, with its close to the side is entirely enlightened and astonishing. Shadow-less, dyed, and level looking, it's not valid for the perception that is a disgrace because, in this stage, it ascends as the sun sets, sets as the sun rises, and it is apparent the entire evening!

Waxing gibbous

In this stage, the moon is entirely enlightened. The sunlight region seems egg-formed (gibbous) and is expanding in size (waxing) every day.

Waning gibbous

The moon's western edge is being devoured by dimness as the evening eliminator materializes. The sunlit, egg-formed region is decreasing (winding down).

First-quarter

This one baffles non-stargazers since it looks like a large portion of a Moon, yet it's called a quarter Moon. That is because the eliminator has finished a quarter (90) of its 360 excursions around the moon. By this rationale, a full Moon ought to be known as a half Moon; however, that is simply senseless, correct? In this stage, the moon ascends around early afternoon and sets at midnight. Along with the eliminator, low-calculated daylight makes long shadows, tossing close by pit and mountains into sharp alleviation ideal for lunar perceptions.

Last quarter

It's seven days and nine hours since the full moon and, presently 90 west of the sun, simply the moon's eastern (left) half is enlightened. At this stage, it ascends at midnight and sets around early afternoon and, similar to the principal quarter stage, offers stunning perspectives.

Waning crescent

With simply the eastern edge sunlit, you'll appreciate a lovely C-formed sickle. Reducing day by day (winding down) will vanish before long as the lunar cycle closes and the moon returns to new. While the moon might keep a similar face to us, it stays a day-by-day changing pleasure to notice.

Lunar liberation

Throughout a lunar cycle, the moon all the while wobbles both latitudinally and longitudinally. These motions are known as freedoms. Freedom in scope gesturing happens because the Moons hub is marginally disposed comparative with Earths, empowering us to peer somewhat over its north and south poles later in the month. Freedom of longitude shaking happens because the moon goes quickest when nearest to earth and slowest when farthest away. Day by day (diurnal), release happens due to our planet's turn. We see the moon according to somewhat alternate points of view when it rises and when it sets. This contextual distinction shows a slight evident revolution in the satellite, first toward the west and afterward toward the east. The consolidated impact of all the above implies that instead of seeing only 50% of the moon, we get to see around 59% over the long run.

Why does the moon have phases?

The moon might seem to change shape; however, the brilliant surface you see and the evening glow that arrives at earth is daylight reflecting off the lunar surface. As the Moon circles our planet, its fluctuating position implies that the sun illuminates various locales, revealing that the moon changes shape over the long run. An ideal method of comprehending the lunar stages is to consistently go out on a crisp evening when the moon is in the sky and notice it. For favoring this, read our aide on the best way to detect the moon. On average, 384,400km from earth, it's shocking to the unaided eye and marvelous through optics or a tiny telescope. It's additionally an incredible objective to photo. For favoring this, read our aide on the best way to photograph the moon or our amateur's manual for astrophotography. The moon appears to be quiet, yet it is rushing toward the east at 3,682 km/h. Since its practical circle is tipped a simple five comparative with Earths, it pretty much follows the ecliptic (The Sun's evident way) across the sky. You might have seen that the moon consistently keeps a similar face turned towards us. This is because it pivots once on its hub while it takes to circle the earth for 27 days and seven hours. This synchronization is called flowing locking. It was an aftereffect of earth's gravitational impact on the youthful moon when it was shaping. During its curved excursion around the earth, the moon travels through stages. The term we use to portray the amount of the lunar circle seems enlightened as seen from the ground. This curved circle joined with the locations is additionally what prompts the presence of a purported supermoon.

The moon is, in every case, half-lit; we just don't view it as such. Whatever stage was seen, the contrary stage is occurring on the furthest side of the moon. And keeping in mind that we just at any point see one eliminator (the name given to the splitting line between the light and dull pieces of the lunar surface) clearing right to the left across the lunar circle whenever there are two of them circumnavigating the Moon precisely 180 separated; the morning eliminator (which introduces the lunar day) and the evening eliminator (which brings the night behind it).

The spiritual significance of the moon phases. The moon is a lovely secret, and it has enraptured the consideration of everybody sooner or later. The moon is an old-fashioned image; it has formed how we follow and get time; it rises each day, acquiring the evening, controls the tides, and is accepted to influence our vigorous fields. It addresses solid, amazing ladylike energy. The moon means astuteness, deception, instinct, and otherworldly association. The Moon cycle interfaces with birth, demise, and resurrection, similar to the seed pattern: it grows up into a blossom, sprouts, and then passes on. We are equipped mainly for adjusting with the Moons energies and initiating our internal power. The lunar cycle is comprised of various stages. Becoming proficient regarding the Moons energies is the initial step along this way, and figuring out how these fantastic energies can be saddled inside your life. We can utilize information about the Moons cycle to reflect inwards at ourselves and our necessities. Every one of the lunar states reflects an alternate part of a profound way that progresses with numerous rehashes and continuous learning. Every one of the Moon Cycles appears unique; it has its exceptional shape and can be spotted without much stretch. Each of these cycles conveys its profound significance and can assist us with streaming with the steadily evolving energies. The moon takes approx. Twenty-eight days to circle the earth, which is how we see a complete cycle consistently. Let's learn about the Moon stages and how we can bridle this power and develop it genuinely.

The moon pivots through 12 stages every month. The fundamental stages generally cantered around in profound work are the new moon, first quarter moon, full moon, and last quarter moon. You might pick which stages resound most. Working with the moon is a natural cycle. While this blog entry will peruse the nuts and bolts, there are various headings once the stages are perceived. Moreover, the center might move with each new moon.

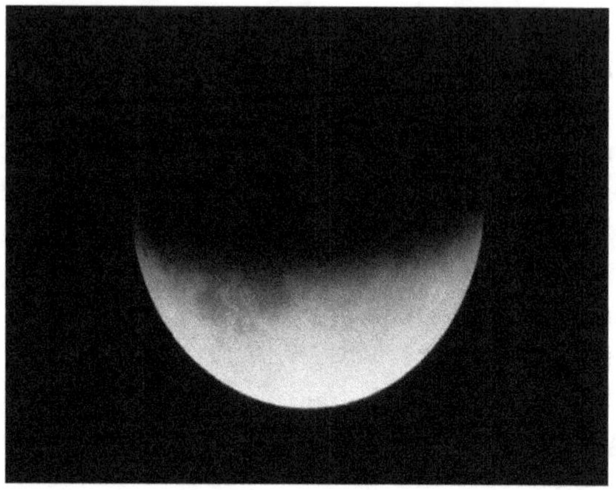

The Spiritual Significance of the Moon Phases

New Moon

The new moon offers a new beginning. This is a period for fresh starts. As of now, we start all over again. It is a period for reflection, rest, and recalibration. This is a period for relinquishing all that is done pursuing our most noteworthy great. We may likewise start to dream about what's to come. We can begin to picture where we might want to be the point at which the moon stage is finished. The haziness of another moon is a period for reflection and investigating the concealed. Frequently considered as a ladylike moon stage, its profound significance is a call for presentations. In being completely present, you can study your most unfathomable longings and genuine wishes that occasionally lose all sense of direction in the whirlwind of so much doing.

New Moon Activities

Reflection is an extraordinary practice for centering the psyche. At the point when the mind is clear, our motivation sparkles splendidly in the bleeding edge of our musings. It might likewise be helpful to diary right now. To focus the body, delicate practice yoga, walk outside, or partake in a calm second with tea.

Waxing Crescent Moon

This is the place where we begin to characterize our objectives and dreams all the more unmistakably. During the waxing sickle moon, we are intellectually preparing for our fantasies. Goals are set that will convey us to the last lunar stage. Right now, indications are made. The allegory customarily utilized for this moon is sowing seeds. We invest energy, longing for what we might want to reap with the last moon stage. However, it isn't the ideal opportunity for activity. Indications mean working with dreams. At the point when we envision what we need as though it has as of now occurred, we permit the universe to get our idea rolling. This likewise allows us to see the work that should be done to accomplish our fantasies.

First Quarter Moon

This is the ideal opportunity for activity! This stage might require hard choices to be made. Zero in on the objectives set during the waxing bow moon. We should stay zeroed in on our fantasies to track down the inward solidarity to win. It may likewise be an opportunity to reconsider the first arrangement. Maybe, new data has been uncovered. Possibly we found unforeseen deterrents. Recall that diversions are essential for the cycle. Pursuits don't need to wreck us! Stay committed to the excursion, paying little heed to any sudden obstructions. Once in a while, the expedition is significantly more remunerating than the objective.

Waxing Gibbous Moon

Our rewards for all the hard work might be beginning to pay off. While it may not be the ideal opportunity to reap, we have a smart thought of how well our seeds will sprout. As of now, we should rehearse appreciation for the little snapshots of achievement. While we are acquiring energy towards our objectives, we should stay watchful simultaneously. Did we neglect anything in the early arranging stages? Accomplishes a person or thing need some additional consideration as of now? The more consideration you give the subtleties at this stage, the more noteworthy result you will accomplish.

Full Moon

During the full moon, everything is enlightened. The moon is sparkling her most splendid in the sky. While the moon is mirroring all the light of the sun, we go inwards to reflect. It very well may be an incredible chance to check in with our objectives and delivery whatever is keeping us down.

Frequently, it is our assumption. Fears around disappointment, dismissal, or weakness can prompt self-destructive behaviour.

Full Moon Activities

Pause for a minute to deliver what is done serving you. Start by journaling or rehearsing contemplation. Contemplation may look like tracking down a peaceful seat or strolling carefully in nature. Likewise, it may be helpful to set any stuck energy free from the body with a delicate yoga practice. To ultimately deliver any bad sentiments, compose a rundown. This rundown can contain stresses, fears, seen disappointments, or individuals/circumstances that have hurt us. Place the rundown in a fire-safe bowl and light it ablaze. Watch the rundown consume and relax. Permit the sentiments to be delivered with the fire.

Waning Gibbous Moon

Try not to be amazed if the feelings delivered during the full moon wait. These things set aside time, mainly if they are established in early connections or long-standing examples of conduct. During the fading gibbous moon, we keep checking how we may be remaining in our specific manner. On the other hand, we might start to see more prominent capacities framing. On this moon, we have a more prominent limit for correspondence, knowledge, and inspiration.

Third Quarter Moon

This is the moon of reaping. We receive the benefits of our devotion. Our objectives are arriving at finishing. Be that as it may, if our goals or accomplishments have not yet happened as expected, something must be acquired. We have likely had incredible achievements, development, or progress all through this moon cycle. This moon requests that we think about how far we have come. Maybe, we are not actually where we wanted to be. Use this opportunity to find what is left to be finished. This isn't a chance to surrender. Discharge any self-restricting convictions. This is a chance to think about our lives in appreciation. We carefully notice our life, our objectives, and our achievements. We can acquire a lot of understanding during this season of reflection.

Third Quarter Moon Activities

Envision noticing your life like a caring passer-by. Maybe, it is an otherworldly being, an individual who loves you genuinely or a creature. This being can see into your heart, psyche, and soul. You have been on an excursion that no other person knows about. You have achieved numerous inside accomplishments that somebody outside of yourself can't perceive. Pause for a minute to commend your inward development. Send yourself a lot of affection, appreciation, and warmth. You are cherished and commendable, paying little heed to your achievements.

Waning Crescent Moon

This is the finishing of the moon cycle. We have one foot previously and the other later on. However, we stand totally in the present. We set aside an effort to check out the objectives we made from the get-go in the moon stages and ponder our advancement. Despite where we are at, we start to give up. This is a period for rest. Permit yourself to remain present. Try not to choose not to move on; that is the place where sadness lives. Try not to stress for the future; that is the place where tension resides. Your tranquillity exists in the present.

The Cycle is Ever-Lasting

The cycle starts again with the new moon. Each new moon is a chance to begin once more. We gain from each stage. Both our difficulties and triumphs characterize how we approach new objectives and assumptions. The moon permits us to follow an aide as we stream all through life. The powers of the moon additionally identify with our inner cycles. For ladies, the moon has a lot of impact on our female cycle. Look at my blog entry The Feminine Cycle and the Moon: It is More Than a Phase for more data.

Working with the Moon

I trust this gave a prologue to the profound meaning of the moon stages. There are countless ways of using this data. Maybe, you just might want to saddle the powers of the moon by defining objectives and showing them into the real world. Moreover, you might use the moon to follow your energy, regenerative cycle, or disposition.

Understanding the myths and mystical energy of the moon phases

We know the periods of the moon influences the tides. As people, our bodies comprise around 60% water, so obviously, the moon affects us, as well! The following are a few different ways you can exploit the distinctive moon stages and her energy. On the off chance that you're a visual student, take a fast look over the above outline from MoonConnection.com. We observe it is beneficial to comprehend the periods of the moon. As an expansive brush outline, each moon cycle is about 29 days. When the moon is new, it's settled between the sun and the earth, so we see its shadow side. As the moon is moving from unknown to complete, it goes through its waxing stage. During the waxing stage, the moon appears to be becoming more significant. The moon is complete when the earth sits between the sun and the moon, so we see it completely lit. As the moon is moving from full-back to new, it goes through its disappearing stage. The moon appears to recoil during this time. As the moon keeps on melting away, it turns into the following new moon.

How to use the moon energy:

Becoming mindful of the moon stages is an extraordinary method for using the energy around you. It likewise fills in as a fantastic approach to regularly check in with yourself (inwardly, intellectually, indeed, profoundly) and put forward objectives appropriately.

New Moon

This is the start of another cycle. Time to sow the seeds of fresh starts and picture your objectives for the impending month. The moon isn't apparent as of now. The energy of this stage can be utilized to line up with the goal. It is about self-revelation and fresh starts. It is an opportunity to get transparency on objectives. It is helpful to approve all through the lunar cycle with the utilization of insistences and reflection on what has been refined, mainly through the responsive stages. The new moon is the second when the Sun and Moon are related, implying that the Sun and Earth are on inverse sides of the moon. At the point when the moon is new, it's the beginning of another moon cycle. With this new beginning, get clear on what you need. It's said to be an extraordinary chance to set aims!

Waxing Moon

This is the start of another cycle. Time to sow the seeds of fresh starts and imagine your objectives for the impending month. The moon isn't noticeable as of now. The energy of this stage can be utilized to line up with expectations. It is about self-disclosure and fresh starts. A chance to get clearness on objectives and it is helpful to approve all through the lunar cycle with the utilization of insistences and reflection on what has been refined, mainly through the responsive stages. The new moon is the second when the Sun and Moon are related, implying that the Sun and Earth are on inverse sides of the moon. At the point when the moon is new, it's the beginning of another moon cycle. With this new beginning, get clear on what you need. It's said to be an incredible opportunity to set intentions. Waxing implies activity make a move on the objectives and expectations you put during the new moon. Dispatch new undertakings, develop new propensities, construct new connections. You will have the developing energy of the moon to fuel you during this 2-week time frame paving the way to the full moon. The significance of this stage is about the obligation to the goal. Understanding your assets and the stuff to push ahead. It is additionally about feeding oneself - and permitting the development to come from a promising circumstance. There is a reflection from the earth to the moon called earth sparkle. The remainder of the moon might be faintly noticeable along these lines. The waxing bow moon is generally apparent after nightfall.

Full Moon

The full moon is an incredible opportunity to get re-established and absorb some unwinding. Approach your aides or holy messengers and slip into sign mode. Wash up, take a stroll in nature. Our feelings are high during this time, after the refreshing waxing stage, so it's essential to rehearse taking care of yourself and being thoughtful. Permit yourself to feel any feelings that emerge and realize that it's typical to handle whatever you encounter. Allow yourself to deliver and let go of whatever overloads you.

Myths and Legends of the Full Moon Phase

The full moon stage has been for quite some time viewed as the stage that causes insane conduct for those on the planet. This has been portrayed in films, network shows, and books is still right up 'til the present time broadly accepted by a scope of people. Yet, this is just one of the numerous fantasies about a sparkling and heavenly full moon! In this article, we examine and, sometimes, expose fantasies and legends of the full moon stage, so you know what's accepted, what's valid, what's as yet unclear.

Ancient Legends of the Full Moon Phase

Let's go on an outing once more into the times past, where a full moon stage was a more puzzling power than it is today! It was accepted referred to that a full moon sparkling splendidly in the sky meant that delightful and clear climate the next day, though a murky or hazy full moon encompassed by a white gleam (also called the radiance of the moon) was an indication that downpour was coming. Another old legend surrounding full moons says that at whatever point a red, straightforward safeguard is available over the circle, it flagged an approaching cataclysmic event, war, or the episode of a plague.

The Moon and our Bodies

There are numerous legends related to a full moon corresponding to our bodies. This is one of the most usually held thoughts regarding this supernatural circle, so it's worth focusing on. Since our bodies are comprised of 75% water, it is said that a full moon has a similar impact on our bodies as it does on the tides of the seas. It likewise noted that a full moon stage prompts more births than some other moon stage. At the same time, science has tracked down no supporting information to back this legend up; it's an old wife's story that is rehashed right up 'til today. Also, many have faith that the full moon impacts ripeness and the monthly cycle. Since the full moon stage and period, both occur consistently. Generally, it was accepted they should be connected. In any case, science has demonstrated over the long haul that these cycles are two separate things, given the way that the lunar cycle is unbendingly set at 29.5 days while a period cycle can differ between 28 to 35 days. Others accept that more epileptic seizures happen during the hour of a full moon stage. While history attests that patients refer to the moon as an energizer for their episodes, a logical examination has not supported this, even though it's generally asserted.

Waning Moon

As the moon closes the cycle and advances from complete to another moon, it's a chance to deliver whatever is done serving you. What are you taking with you into the following month? What would you like to relinquish or abandon? This 2-week time span is ideal for thoughtfulness and reflection. Take some time alone to consider the past 20ish days and note what worked and what didn't. Which expectations should be changed or refreshed? Set aside some effort to diary on what was helpful and what was pernicious over the previous month.

Gibbous Moon - Waxing

Right now, 50% of the moon is illuminated. The Sunlit part lit is gradually getting more significant. Waxing means incrementing progressively. The time frame in which the apparent surface of the moon increments. What is working for yourself and what isn't? Essential minutes here in the energy stream of the whole cycle. Dispose of what isn't lining up with needs and refine your interaction. The waxing gibbous moon happens between the principal quarter and the full moon. The sun enlightens the more significant part of the moon's surface during this period.

Disseminating Moon - Waning Gibbous

The moon isn't entirely enlightened by daylight. The piece of the moon this is lit up is gradually getting more modest. The importance of disappearing is to get progressively more modest. Fading (of the moon) identifies with the period during which the apparent surface of the moon diminishes after the full moon comes to the fading moon. The energy here is extraordinary. Coordinate new points of view and adjust vision to sentiments. The time frame between a full moon and the second from last quarter is called a gibbous moon. The piece of the moon enlightened goes down from complete to half during this period.

Last Quarter - Waning Quarter Moon

A big part of the moon is brightened by the sun. The amount that we can see enlightened is gradually getting more modest. The second from last quarter Moon happens when the other portion of the moon is enlightened analyzed the primary quarter. This time is about the energy of moving towards the acknowledgment of a fruitful result. Taking the necessary steps to wrap up. On the actual second day from last quarter, the moon rises in the evening and sets in the day.

Balsamic Moon - Waning Crescent

A little piece of the moon is enlightened now. Every second it is getting more modest and more modest. The melting away sickle moon is between the second from last quarter moon and the following new moon. Time to refocus. An intelligent mark of energy - a period for consideration. Reevaluate, venture fresh. Assess. Before long, an ideal opportunity to begin once more. The moon is generally apparent before nightfall. The sun enlightens not precisely a large portion of the moon during this period. It very well might be feasible to see earth gleam on the clouded side of the moon when just a tiny part of the moon is apparent.

The relationship between Moon phases, rituals, and spells.

While the moon has its sorcery, appearance is a cycle. Your most huge longings don't just show up for the time being; they set aside time, and you should believe that planning. Checking out the periods of the moon gives a structure to go to again and again. What's more, it can engage you to discover a genuine sense of reconciliation and comprehension in the unfurling of your lives. Perhaps an ideal method for associating with the moon and utilizing its energy is with a moon custom.

The Modern Moon Ritual

Moon ceremonies are an antiquated and hallowed practice that began in Egypt, Babylonia, India, and China, where moon love was a piece of the way of life. The periods of the moon impact the development or decay of plants, creatures, and human existence. Along these lines, lolling in the twilight was viewed as a hallowed and fundamental piece of each cycle. Today, the ceremonial moon conveys the same holiness and carries a delightfully base practice into the advanced world. It's something we frantically need in our continually taking a gander at a-screen lifestyle and when life itself is frequently loaded up with difficulties, grievousness, and despair. The lovely thing about customs, mainly those identified with the moon, is that they welcome you to get peace. They request you to sow seeds from the goal and be unified with nature. Ideally, liberated from interruptions. And keeping in mind that there are eight periods of the moon, the most potent stages are the new moon and the full moon.

Understanding How to Manifest with The Moon Via The 8 Phases of The Moon
The new moon

This happens when the sun and moon come into the arrangement; when the sun's yang (manly) energy converges with the yin (female) embodiment of the moon, and the moon ascends with the sun at first light. The moon and the sun conjoin in the sky (adjust at a similar degree celestially) during this stage, so we don't see the moon. This is the beginning of another lunation and its opportunity to get still and sow new want seeds. During another moon, it serves us to inhale new life into any space of stagnation or any spot in your life where you might want to affect positive change. This is the ideal opportunity to set a goal to show with the moon.

The waxing crescent moon

During the days that follow another moon, when the moon starts to ascend after the sun, its opportunity to moor into your expectations. Zero in on one thing you need to bring into reality during this lunar cycle. Keeping that in mind, practice perceptions and insistences as of now. Work your new moon expectation out obviously and compactly, and read it day by day. Doing this will assist you with showing with the moon.

The waxing quarter moon

Right now is an ideal opportunity to take a gander at the difficulties you presently face and settle on choices concerning how you need to continue. This is the hour of the moon cycle when the sun and the moon square one another. A court in soothsaying is when two divine bodies structure a 90-degree point. This permits you to see the issues that have emerged since the new moon and empowers you to change your arrangements appropriately. Face misfortune with an unfaltering brain. Find workarounds. Work gainfully with challenges. They are your most prominent educators and a vital piece of showing with the moon.

The waxing gibbous moon

This high-energy second, just before the full moon, offers a viewpoint. With the lunar energy waxing to the top, things should begin to feel like they are adjusting. Subsequently, this is an ideal opportunity to increase the energy in your life. Make an enormous move for your planned craving. Follow what you need to show with the moon sincerely.

The full moon

Fundamentally, full moons are supporting. Consider it: the moon, symbolic of the female, gets the sun's light, sparkling it back to us with brightening. When the moon is full, its solid gravitational draw on the earth makes for a period of pinnacle inventive energy and unbelievably amazing instinctive forward leaps. In any case, considerably more thus, since the full moon rises when the sun sets, the two lights effortlessly the sky simultaneously making for intense time. The full moon emphasizes the aims set during its waxing stage. Set aside an effort to consider what the full moon raises for you. Get outside around evening time and let the light of the moon sparkle upon you. Then, at that point, take your consideration back to what you need to show with the moon. What requirements to move for you to carry your objective to fulfillment?

The waning gibbous moon

After the full moon, while the moon's light melts away, it's fundamental to consider what you want to deliver. During this stage, ponder what is hindering you from accepting your ideal result. Give close consideration to any fiery breaks or barriers keeping you away from communicating the realization of your perfect outcome. Embrace the straightforwardness and let go of what's obstructing you from having what you need.

The waning quarter moon

At the point when the moon starts to disappear and the light scatters, there is a call to go inside and accomplish the interior work of looking for answers and heart-driven direction. Award yourself full authorization to respect your sentiments during this stage. Especially during this time, your feelings are encoded with messages regarding where we want to make some noise or changes in our lives. Listen eagerly for heading and direction. It's a chance to shed what's keeping you away from showing your craving for the moon.

The waning crescent moon

This presents the last period of the whole moon cycle. It happens just before the following new moon. It gives a chance to think about back the entire lunar cycle that has occurred. What have you realized? What has occurred? What hasn't? Rehash your new moon expectation and assess how you've changed since you composed it. Then, at that point, consider how you need to get rearranged for this next new moon.

A New Moon Ritual: Manifest with the Moon

The new moon is a clear page, a new beginning, a second to turn internal and consider what we need to call into our lives and what we want to relinquish. It's without a doubt a period for rest and reflection so that the ideal customer would be in the solace of your own home.

How to Begin:

1. Set the environment.

Before participating in any custom, spotless and arranging your space, repairing and discarding chaos builds up the energy for the assistance. I like to burn through incense, light a fire, turn on moderating music, and chill. I keep several pieces of heavenly paper and a pen nearby for forming.

2. Conjure a connection to the Divine.

Call upon an association with the source energy you feel upholds you the most: guides, heavenly messengers, or some other heavenly association. By and by, I like to associate with every one of the four components: air, fire, water, and earth. Then, at that point, I honor the Sun and Moon.

3. Sit comfortably and write.

Snatch those bits of paper and record the things in your day-to-day existence you either wish to bring in or are prepared to deliver. This could be sure sentiments, fears, or barriers anything you know isn't serving you for sure you need to call into your life. This could be an open position, a relationship, more monetary plenitude, an adventure; you name it.

4. Declare.

The following stage is to peruse your desires, the stuff you need to call into your life now out loud. Talking them out loud assumes an essential part in rejuvenating them. You might see that they inspire considerably more feeling when spoken, and that feeling is fundamental for indication.

5. Meditate and complete.

Presently that you've let go and accounted for what you genuinely want, sit unobtrusively, follow your breath, and picture your cravings are working out as expected. Set the expectation to remain open to these components and encounters entering your life and some other development openings you might require en route. You can either do this custom performance or welcome others to go along with you as a reference. While doing it single-handedly is excellent, likewise something convincing about is being heard and held by those you love, so they, as well, can hold your longings for you and the other way around.

A Full Moon Ritual: Manifest with the Moon

When the full moon shows up, it's an opportunity to make space to check out what has and hasn't happened as expected right now; a full moon custom is an opportunity to get peaceful, reflect, and celebrate. In contrast to the new moon, the full moon addresses productivity and fulfillment and carries a ton of energy.

Here's how to approach your ritual:

1. Get cantered.

Since there is a reasonably considerable amount of energy present, it's best to figure out how to bring serenity into your space so that you can saddle the energy to your advantage. Take a couple of purifying breaths, line up with your area, and chill.

2. Write it out.

Pause for a minute to consider the beyond a couple of weeks. What has unfolded? Where are the victories? What are you knocking toward? Where do you see openings for development and extension?

3. Release and Declare.

Once you've explained what's worked out as expected and what hasn't, it's an opportunity to record and deliver what is hindering the encounters that haven't shown up yet. You can either ritualistically wash these composed hindrances or squares away for good or consume them in a fire-safe vessel.

4. Take a moon bath.

Assuming that you can get outside and allow the evening glow to contact your skin. Very much like our bodies need Vitamin D from daylight, we likewise benefit from moonlight. It's said to assist with decreasing aggravation and is known to help our monthly cycles.

5. Dance it out.

Regardless of whether you're celebrating or as yet bringing in your fantasies (recollect, it doesn't happen out of the blue!). Dance to your cherished music to move any stale energy out of your body and give more gentility and pleasure inside. Cutting out space during both of these moon stages to go internal and check out what's appearing for you set out the freedom to make aims and track down rhythmicity in your own life.

CHAPTER 3
MOON RITUAL/SPELLS

A deep understanding of moon rituals and spells.

The moon has consistently been recognized as a divine body that connects to our feelings through the ages. Various religions place significance on the moon. These religions range from agnostic to coordinated religion. The moon's lunar cycle is frequently utilized to stamp schedules and explicit ceremonies related to each moon stage. Like its regular partner, the sun, the moon likewise has many divine beings and goddesses connected to it. Also, the many fantasies and legends loping around the moon. Have you at any point utilized the expression very rarely, or should there be a full moon around evening time? Indeed, those are a couple of instances of how the moon was alluded to working out time and attached to explicit feelings.

But why are different moon phases critical?

There are energies related to various moon stages. Everyone is incredible for using explicit customs and spells.

New Moon Phase

This moon stage is the start of a lunar cycle. There will be a few evenings when the moon appears to have vanished totally from the sky a month. During this time, the moon takes cover behind the sun for a couple of days. This present time would be the best opportunity to perform spells that require aim. Assuming you need to start another propensity or add one more supplication to your custom, this particular moon stage is likewise the ideal setting to begin.

A quick candle ritual that you can do simply requires:

- One (1) white candle*
- A bowl of water
- Salt
- Two bits of paper

1. On one piece of paper, compose what you mean to give up for the month while, on the other, something that you wish to develop. This can be anything from another propensity to an objective that you want to accomplish before the month's over.

2. In an open space, start by salting the water in the bowl. Place the white candle in its middle, make sure to have the candle's wick over the water.

3. Burn the two bits of paper, beginning with the one you wish to give up. Douse the paper in the salted water. Make sure to keep the flame lit all through the custom.

Waxing Moon

The moon in the waxing moon stage resembles a retrogressive C. This stage happens as the sun moves gradually from behind the moon. As the moon develops fuller, it's a visual portrayal of the moon assembling its powers. This is likewise the stage known in the Triple Moon Goddess image as the Maiden. This is mainly when the goddess is in her gullible state toward the start of Her excursion; this is an incredible chance to zero in on self-revelation or a spell that spotlights personal growth. This is the energy frequently connected with this stage. Is it true that you are a chronic organizer or trust that the ideal opportunity will begin a venture? Waxing moon stages are most certainly an opportunity to plan the remainder of your month and investigate your imagination.

Waxing Moon Intention Spell

- One (1) bay leaf
- A small fireproof cauldron or container

1. Stand by a window where you can see the waxing moon. Assuming you're adequately fortunate to have an undisturbed clearing outside, that is great. Set up your flame-resistant holder.
2. Write your plan on the cove leaf, make sure to zero in on this expectation unmistakably to you as you do as such. This can be something dull as well, such as

improving as a craftsman, for instance. You could likewise utilize a solitary word to address your goal.

3. Thank the moon for being in its waxing stage by raising your free palms to the moon, inlet leaf still in your grasp. Then, at that point, press the sound leaf over your heart, accepting a couple of full breaths as you imagine your expectation being satisfied.

4. Once you feel you've grounded yourself and made an association with the moon, consume the leaf in your compartment. Picture your purpose ascending with the smoke towards the moon.

5. Accept and accept that the moon has accepted your goal, and sit tight for the leaf to wear out.

First Quarter Moon

The primary quarter moon and second from last quarter moon stage are comparable. They are both enlightened partially through. This happens because the sun is one next to the other with the moon. The moon has arrived at a significant portion of its power during these two stages. The primary quarter stage enlightens on the right side, while the second from the last quarter is left.

The primary quarter stage is incredible for internal reflection and considering what is around you. Set aside the effort to commend your accomplishments. It is additionally a phenomenal chance to begin arranging ceremonies for the full moon stage. The laws of drawing in material articles are most grounded during this period as well. Show these articles by journaling.

Waxing Gibbous Moon

In case you have an errand you've been battling to finish, the waxing gibbous moon stage is an incredible time for you to get that little push of energy. This is the moon stage when a fragment of the dim moon is seen on the uttermost left edge of the moon. The power encompassing this stage is care. Any custom enchantment done in this stage should circle efficiency or maintain your inward feelings and feelings impacted by outside environmental factors. While you can lead ceremonies during this stage, an extraordinary method for utilizing this specific moon stage is investing energy into your arrangements. Zero in on the goal you had set with the Waxing Moon Intention spell and trust that the universe is getting ready to satisfy it.

Full Moon

This is additionally the stage known in the Triple Moon Goddess image as the mother. It is the epitome of affection and fruitfulness. This stage welcomes you to give and get love. To most rehearsing Wiccans and agnostics, this is the most potent type of supernatural energy found. It's for sure a definitive chance to perform spells that identify with signs. It's even a fun time for expulsion ceremonies. This is an incredible time if you have a specific interest in divination and sharpening your clairvoyant capacities. The full moon is the most remarkable energy you can need to fuel your powers. If you don't have a specific objective as a main priority but might want to exploit the full moons controls, you can endeavor this fundamental ceremony.

Full Moon Wish Spell

- One (1) white candle*
- Pen and paper
1. Light the white flame and spot on a flame-resistant tile.
2. Gaze at the highest point of the fire and spotlight on your relaxing. Take three (3) full breaths.
3. Chant, Tonight, I decide to mirror your light and open myself to your brilliant clearness. I get this fire going for the sake of the moon, so my solicitation might be conceded. Much thanks to you, goddess, for I have brought your Blessing and Vision by the light of a fire. Thus, bit it be.
4. On your piece of paper, compose your desire and make it as nitty-gritty and explicit as could be expected.
5. Once the light quenches itself out, keep the piece of paper in a protected, dry spot.

6. Scrape the wax and either cover or discard it since your plan is currently set.

Waning Gibbous Moon

As the moon loses its power, it begins to obscure on the right side. This is likewise the last stage found in the Triple Moon Goddess image, known as the Crone. The Crone is the goddess in her most seasoned structure, brimming with intelligence. She recognizes that She is wilting ceaselessly and turns into an update that death is just essential for the pattern of life. Without end, there can't be birth.

Since the moon is starting to lose its energy, this is an extraordinary opportunity to zero in on fully acknowledging yourself. If you have a custom based on conquering deterrents, this would be an ideal opportunity to perform it. Some additionally suggest making a stride back and being contemplative during this moon stage. It assists with distinguishing trouble spots in your day-to-day existence that need a center. Once differentiated, you can lay out your aims and objectives for the following month.

An ideal purifying custom to perform during this time is one that includes tie enchantment.

Banishing Knot Magic Spell

- A dark harmony around 13 crawls long
- Dragon's blood fundamental oil

- A little piece of paper
1. On the piece of paper, compose what you wish to oust. This can likewise be depicted in a solitary word.
2. Tie a free bunch toward one side of the harmony. Before you fix it totally, glance through the opening and read your purpose on the piece of paper. Picture it vanishing from your life.
3. Tighten the bunch, then, at that point, trickle a solitary drop of the fundamental oil on the bunch. As you do this, say, I do tie you and oust you from my life.
4. Repeat stages 2 and 3 for five additional occasions until you have a sum of six bunches.
5. Keep your harmony in a protected place and forget about it.
6. Throw the piece of paper away since your aim is currently set.

Third Quarter Moon

As referenced previously, this is the point at which the moon enlightens precisely part of the way through. Just 50% of its left side can be seen. This is a visual portrayal of the moon at a significant portion of its power. Assuming you've been reflecting during the fading gibbous stage, then, at that point, you ought to have a thought of what necessities are eliminated from your life. The second from last quarter moon is the ideal time to offer back in the wake of absorbing the moon's energy. Consider the most recent couple of days by journaling. Record any bad examples that you need to break.

Waning Moon

This stage is when the last bit of the moon is noticeable on the farthest left side. The moon has spent the remainder of its power and gives up to nature's cycle at this stage. Assuming you have not accomplished the objectives you've set toward the start of the month, don't beat yourself up over it. The winding down moon stage is likewise about self-generosity. We suggest delivering negative energy during this stage. Zero in on your weaknesses and antagonism. This energy discharge varies a little from the arrival of pessimism during the second from last quarter moon.

Eliminating Obstacles from Your Life Spell

- One (1) red candle*
- Olive Oil
- Salt and pepper
- Cayenne pepper
- Pen and paper
- Sage (optional)
- Black cloth (optional)

1. To start, track down an open space under the moon. Purify your things with sage.

2. Ground yourself through reflection and breathing to feel associated.
3. On the paper, compose the snag that has been in your manner.
4. Fold the paper multiple times, trying to get collapsing far from you. As you do, rehash so anyone might hear the particular aim you composed on the paper.
5. Pour a little olive oil on the tips of your fingers, then, at that point, rub it on the flame, in a descending movement away from the wick.
6. Place your collapsed paper under the as of late dressed light.
7. Sprinkle a circle of salt around your flame and say, I favor this salt to purge and eliminate any blockages in my way.
8. Sprinkle a circle of pepper straightaway and say, I charge this pepper to kill anything in the method of me and [your goal].
9. Lastly, take your cayenne pepper and sprinkle a third external circle around the salt and pepper. As you do this, I engage this cayenne pepper to impact away all obstructions in my manner.
10. Light the flame and say a supplication to your benefactor God or Goddess. Invest some energy envisioning the impediment crumbling from your life.
11. When the candle has torched as far as possible (or near it), blow it out and

> envelop it with the dark material and keep it in a protected spot.

Dark Moon

Most witches set aside this effort to re-energize their otherworldly energies in this stage. Some appreciate saddling the dull energy related to the dim moon. This is the point at which some would think about the conclusion to the lunar cycle. Wizardry customs have done in this stage revolve around getting out from under damaging propensities.

Protection spells are also something one might consider during this moon phase.

A fast security spell that you can do simply utilizes a solitary fixing favoured dark salt or coarse white salt. Sprinkle this around the edge of your home, at the entryways and windowsills. This makes dividers of assurance against negative energies that may attempt to enter your home. You can likewise purchase instant assurance oil made of a mix of fundamental oils. Touch this at the side of your entryways and windows.

Harnessing the mystical energy of the moon

1. Make purposeful time for yourself to associate with the energy of the full moon. Whether you invest this energy alone or with a gathering of companions that share a similar expectation, this is

the most fundamental thing you can do. At the point when the moon is complete, and you make a purposeful chance to associate, it permits the moon's energy to travel through you and present to all of your kinds of advantages, going from soul-level recuperating to showing powers to getting clearness on your following stages throughout everyday life.

2. Look into what celestial sign the full moon is in. This will assist you with focusing and remaining on the ball, so you can explore the ground-breaking season of each full moon with mindfulness and tackle its power! Each full moon has its remarkable crystal gazing, which can assist you with seeing precisely what the specific energy of the new moon is. For instance, a full moon in Libra is an incredible opportunity to mend connections. In contrast, a full moon in Taurus gives stable, grounded energy with the goal that you can think about your monetary and wellness objectives. Comprehending this will uphold you in making your goals and moulding the regions you will zero in on in your contemplations, activities, and full moon ceremonies. The full moon's energy is incredibly intense in case its mysterious sign lines up with your visionary sun sign, as this will probably be the evening of the year that has the most power for you.

3. Set clear goals. When you set your dreams on the full moon, they add additional energy to convey them to realization. An incredible practice to add to

your expectations is to shut your eyes and envision and feel the aim like it is now finished. With the light of the full moon radiating brilliantly above you, feel into what your entire being genuinely wants. Record it, talk it so anyone can hear, and certify them emphatically. Simply make sure to be cautious about what you wish for - it might just materialize!

4. Contemplate. There is a wide range of reflection styles, and your instinct can direct you to what exactly is best for you on each full moon. Regardless of whether you decide to sit upright and notice your breathing, set down and pay attention to shamanic drumming, dance, paint, take a walk, or even wash your dishes with mindfulness - decide to implant this time with your total presence, clear your brain, and tune in. The full moon enlightens portions of ourselves we didn't know about previously, which can incorporate acknowledgment about ourselves and our lives and dreams of our subsequent stages.

5. Diary. You can decide to diary about your feelings (which are typically uplifted by the moon), your profound excursion, your musings, expectations, or whatever is alive for you. Journaling is a device that brings profound lucidity and a-ha minutes because rather than contemplations whirling around within our heads, we can express what is available. It puts together and grounds the extraordinary energy to make congruity and recuperating. In doing this, we can

develop emphatically rather than turning into a casualty to the uplifted point of the full moon. Journaling assists us with becoming cognizant makers of our lives; it helps us remember our ability to pick confidence and sympathy rather than oblivious examples. It generally brings mindfulness, and that is a significant stage on the excursion of mending.

6. Place your precious stones in the evening glow to scrub and charge. If you do not just need to encounter the force of the full moon during the evening of the full moon itself, however, you need to proceed with the mending and change consistently, place your precious stones in the twilight to scrub and charge them. Likewise, you can explore different avenues regarding setting a gem under your cushion when you rest, washing with them, or conveying one with you in your pocket. Gems can be utilized for some techniques for mending.

7. Do a full moon custom. This is energetically suggested assuming that you are bringing in change and self-development! For some time, the full moon has been viewed as a solid opportunity to do customs for indication, recuperating, profound direction, and expanding individual power. Moreover, the full moon can be used towards worldwide recovery - particularly within sight of sisterhood. Gathering with different ladies in a Sister Circle on the full moon is an old practice that

helps each lady join in and swell out to contact her family, her local area, and Mother Earth herself.

How to prepare for moon spells (A step-by-step approach)

Utilizing the moon eases in your enchanted will add a lot of capacity to your ceremonies. The moon requires 29 1/2 days to go through one of its cycles, and each stage has its particular energy. This ceremonial arrangement with the New or Waxing Moon. You can decide to recognize this when it is genuinely new during the Dark of the Moon or when you see the principal sickle in the evening sky.

(Part 1) Readying Your Gathering Space

1). Choose a fitting setting for your custom. New Moon ceremonies are usually drilled by the people who partner themselves with enchantment, agnosticism, black magic, yoga, contemplation, or some other sort of otherworldly mindfulness. The area you pick will preferably be outside. Being outside implies you will be associated with the rest of the world, making it more straightforward to bridge the energy of nature. Assuming that being outside is absurd, ensure you are in an agreeable room where you won't be upset.

2). Cleanse the region. Purging the part is critical to preparing it for the new moon custom. You can do these in one of two different ways. One way is by smirching the area sage is ideal as it's related with the moon. You can likewise scrub the area by lighting incense. Some successful incense types related to the new moon incorporate lavender, lemon demulcent, and calamus fragrances. To smirch the region, shine the finish of the savvy stick and blow on it until there is a noticeable seething sparkle. Wave it around your body and around the space where your customs will be performed.

3). Set up a particular stepped area. You can design it so much or as little as you wish; it's everything up to your very own inclinations. Put a beautiful embroidered artwork on the ground with a pad around it for every member in the custom. Make your particular stepped area on top of the woven artwork. Incorporate things that associate you to nature (like blossoms) and things that bury the hatchet (like incense or some nostalgic knickknack). Use something to relate with the components: a quill or fragrance for air; a shell or little bowl of water for water; a stone or limited quantity of soil for the earth; and, at long last, a light (white or silver for the moon) to address shoot.

4). Choose a fitting setting for your custom. New Moon ceremonies are usually drilled by the people who partner themselves with enchantment, agnosticism, black magic, yoga, contemplation, or some other sort of otherworldly mindfulness. The area you pick will preferably be outside. Being outside implies you will be associated with the rest of the world, making it more straightforward to bridge the energy of nature.

If being outside is unimaginable, ensure you are in an agreeable room where you won't be upset.

(Part 2) Choosing Your Moon Ritual

1). Decide on your goal for the custom. The New Moon is an incredible opportunity to make a fresh start, request another affection, start a course of mending, or restore your obligation to an old goal. Record several words or expressions that reflect what you desire to escape the custom.

2). Choose a few words for the custom. Assuming you wish, you can get ready or exploration a few words that you will say during the tradition. These words can be a contribution of appreciation or a confident wish for what's to come. Say anything you desire. The fact is to associate with nature and to individuals around you.

- Assuming you need to propose your appreciation to nature, take a stab at saying something like this: Dear Mother Earth, she gives life and light to us all; thank you for the plentiful favors you have presented to us.
- Assuming you need to request a particular longing to become a reality, take a stab at saying something like this: I come here today to propose my solicitation to the universe so that it may turn into my reality.
- If you are playing out the customs with more than one individual, you should offer

every member a chance to examine their expectations along these lines.

3). Include something to assist with setting the disposition. During your New Moon custom, you need to feel revitalized and invigorated. Discussing a sonnet or singing a melody is an extraordinary method for going into the right outlook for the custom

(Part 3) Performing Your Moon Ritual

1) Acknowledge the energy of the components. Call upon the power of every element and its comparing course. Fire is in the South, Water in the West, Earth in the North, and Air in the East.

- Note: The relating headings change contingent upon your exact way.
- Say something like; I call upon the energy of the components to help me in my excursion. Fire in the South, Water in the West, Earth in the North, and Air in the East.
- Consider presenting a message that commends the things you partner with each bearing.

2) Recite your words. When you experience arriving at a position of harmony, right now is an ideal opportunity to peruse or say a couple of words that mirror your expectation. If you wish, you can consume the paper on which you composed those words/phrases in the fire of a flame. As it consumes, envision your words/goals being completed and with the smoke into the universe.

- Assuming you can't arrive at a position of harmony on account of something disturbing you, this moment would likewise be a decent opportunity to recognize this. Envision what is causing you agony or stress and is being out of hand from you by the smoke from the candle.
- Assuming that you are playing out your New Moon custom in a gathering, offer every individual a chance to peruse their aims and consume the paper in the candles flares.

3) Perform a representative demonstration. This is an incredible expansion to recognizing your goals since it permits you to genuinely envision what you want. Make the emblematic demonstration yourself and go ahead and get innovative.

4) Share your goals with others. Assuming others are present at your New Moon custom, pause for a minute for everybody to impart a portion of their expectations to the gathering. This will assist you with interfacing with each other. However, it will likewise give more energy to every people aim

5) Thank the energies. This will assist you with shutting the door on every one of the components you have called upon. Each gathering part should close the service such that it feels fitting for them. An ideal method for shutting a custom is to present one of the accompanying expressions:

- Also, none its Harm, Enhance My Charm.
- By the Power of Three, So Mote It Be.
- Favored Be.

Conclusion

The Moon is Earth's just regular satellite. She goes with and impacts us in numerous ways, regardless of whether we can't consistently see it. Most Witches are amazingly touchy to the lunar cycles and can detect the moon's impact and stages on them. This can be utilized to settle on better choices and anticipate better outcomes thus. It has been demonstrated that the moon's periods have various impacts and effects on the earth and every single living being. The lunar stages can change the sea tides, the climate, our rest designs, our states of mind, and numerous different things, including paces of richness, brought about by the additional light that the full moon gives

From the beginning of time, savvy ladies and men were very much aware of the force of the moon and its evolving stages and created spells and customs that changed following exploiting this energy as could be expected.

Best Spells to Cast on Each Moon

The moon's periods are eight, and we can bunch them into four fundamental stages: New (Dark) Moon, Waxing Moon, Full Moon, and Waning Moon. Let us see what the rest are and what they can mean for your magic by learning the best spells to project during each lunar stage.

The eight periods of the moon are: new moon, Waxing Crescent, First Quarter, Waxing Gibbous, Full Moon, Waning Gibbous, Last Quarter, and Waning Crescent

1. New Moon

This is the main period of the lunar cycle. It begins when the moon is undetectable (this state goes on for one day and is otherwise called a Dark Moon) since it rests between the sun and the earth. In the following days, the moon gradually starts to show up in the sky. The energy of the New Moon is related to thoughtfulness, self-examination, and reflection on ourselves. A chance for a new beginning and a New You.

What to do during the New Moon

New Moon Spells

The energies of this Moon stage aren't truly going to build your powers of Manifestation. Rather than enchanting in the New Moon, utilizes this opportunity to build up an overall expectation for the lunar cycle that starts today. Work on your own space: clean your custom region, begin or enliven your Book of Shadows, look into spells on the web, or scrub down. Think about your desires and wants, yet additionally on your questions and fears. Plan and ponder all that you need to imagine and accomplish during the following 28 days!

2. Waxing Crescent

This moon period begins three days after the New Moon when you can start to see a little piece of the moon in obscurity sky. The sickle moon is the image and portrayal of the Wiccan Goddess, typifying Manifestation and Abundance.

What to do during the Waxing Crescent Moon

Waxing-Crescent-Moon-Spells

Cast a spell that will assist you with developing your business or your vocation. This is a happy time for the long haul or material-gain spells, for example, a cash drawing spell or a custom for getting another line of work. Zero in on your work, and you're schooling. Abstain from considering your objectives something later on but instead as something previously beginning to occur. Likewise, charge your Moon Water on the Waxing Crescent Moon.

3. First Quarter

This stage starts around seven days after the new moon. This is an excellent opportunity to make a move concerning your most profound wishes and to address your most significant blockages. It is an extraordinary time for development and self-recuperating. As a continuation of the last stage, the energies present can assist you with feeling more precise and more mindful of how your instinct and second qualities are created.

What to do during the First Quarter Moon

First Quarter Moon Rituals

Utilize the energies of this stage to mend on both otherworldly and enthusiastic levels. As the moon is filling in shape, you can zero in on self-development. It's a period of wealth, so use it imaginatively, permit the right things, and individuals come to you and draw in the significant things that you wish to see a tremendous amount of. Complete wellbeing and excellence medicines center around self-awareness like expanding confidence and self-esteem, family and richness, and work on fostering your Powers of Manifestation. Cast these spells during a First Quarter moon:

4. Waxing Gibbous

This is the fourth moon stage. It begins the tenth day after the New Moon and goes on until the thirteenth day after it. It is a chance to show restraint. Perceive the force of the universe and let it take control. Stop your activities and, on second thought, notice the state where your undertakings are. Unwind, break down, and plan your best course of action.

What to do during the Waxing Gibbous Moon

Waxing-Gibbous-Moon-Rituals

Pause and foster persistence. Assuming that you have begun enchanting during the past moon stages, this is an ideal opportunity to hold on and let the universe go about its business. This is an incubation period where we don't truly need to do anything specifically. Utilize this chance to prepare for the following stage:

5. Full Moon

It happens 14 days after the New Moon, and it's simple to recognize because the night sky is out of nowhere gleaming surrounding you. Gaze upward, and you'll observe a significant pearl sparkling as it reflects daylight upon the earth. It addresses the zenith and achievement of all that you began during the Waxing moon stage. Presently everything is in its completion. During this stage, individuals are more responsive, and social connections become ideal.

What to do during the Full Moon

Full Moon Rituals and Witch Spells

It happens 14 days after the New Moon, and it's simple to distinguish because the night sky is abruptly gleaming surrounding you. Turn upward, and you'll observe a significant pearl sparkling splendidly as it reflects daylight upon the earth. It addresses the zenith and achievement of all that you began during the Waxing moon stage. Presently everything is in its completion. During this stage, individuals are more responsive, and social connections become more favorable. The full moon favors correspondence and social association. This stage is entirely ideal for managing heartfelt issues, as it very well may be a genuine sexual enhancer. Assuming you have been dealing with an affection spell, this is the point at which you will see the best outcomes. Follow up on your cravings and take risks! As this moon upgrades correspondence with the otherworldly world, any custom performed under the Full Moon will encounter an increase in power. Divination ceremonies are particularly fortified by this moon, similar to any close-to-home spell work that could utilize a significant lift, including customs for plenitude, insurance, love, or guile. Your odds of coming out on top are more prominent than during some other lunar stage. Utilize the force of the full moon to project any kind of spell with certainty.

6. Waning Gibbous

It begins the third day after the Full Moon until the seventh day after that. It carries a chance to eliminate and dispose of negative energies. Utilize this moon stage to liberate yourself from loads that are keeping you down.

What to do during the Waning Gibbous Moon

Banishing rituals and any spells to dispose of negative things and circumstances are leaned toward this moon stage. For instance, those identified with separation, detachment, expulsion, addictions, stress, and other negative sentiments.

7. Last Quarter

This stage begins the seventh day after the Full Moon and continues until the tenth day, a short time later. Let the energy of this moon unobtrusively finish your expulsion processes and scrubs. Close any forthcoming issues and unobtrusively restore your inward powers.

What to do during the Last Quarter Moon

The time has come to be wary and utilize this lunar stage to rest. You can likewise use this chance to eliminate yourself from ruinous connections, harmful standards of conduct, or anything hurtful in your life. Defeat despairing and melancholy. A few Witches utilize this moon stage to project spells for equity or against adversaries.

8. Waning Crescent

This is the last period of the Moon cycle. It ranges from the tenth day after the Full Moon until the night before the New Moon. It's a snapshot of conclusion and reflection, don't utilize it to settle on any significant choices or start another undertaking.

What to do during the Waning Crescent Moon

Express appreciation for a cycle that finishes, permitting another one to start. Think back to what you have achieved during the previous month, what ruins you made, and how you can improve and continue to develop. Perform ceremonies of appreciation and unwinding, which show end.

82